TWENTY GREAT PAINTINGS

A short introductory tour

NATIONAL GALLERY PUBLICATIONS
LONDON

The National Gallery
Admission free

Open
Monday to Saturday, 10.00 am–6.00 pm
Sunday, 2.00–6.00 pm

Closed
New Year's Day, Good Friday, May Day, Christmas Eve,
Christmas Day and Boxing Day

The National Gallery Shops and Information Desks
Open: Monday to Saturday, 10.00 am–5.40 pm
Sunday, 2–5.40 pm

Micro Gallery: Computer Information Room
Open: Monday to Saturday, 10.00 am–5.30 pm
Sunday, 2–5.30 pm

Lectures, Films and Guided Tours
Lunchtime slide lectures and films are held in the
Sainsbury Wing Theatre throughout the year. Details of
these, guided tours and other special events held in the
Gallery can be obtained from the Information Desks, and
are listed in the current issue of the *National Gallery News*.

© National Gallery Publications Limited 1991

Published in Great Britain in 1991 by
National Gallery Publications Limited
5/6 Pall Mall East, London SW1Y 5BA
Reprinted 1993
British Library Cataloguing in Publication Data

Twenty great paintings.
  1. Oil Paintings. Europe
  759.94074

  ISBN 0–947645–95–0

Printed and bound by Butler and Tanner Limited,
Frome and London

FRONT COVER Titian, *Bacchus and Ariadne* (No. 8, detail).

CONTENTS

1. English or French School(?) (*c*.1395)
The Wilton Diptych

Egg tempera on oak, each panel 47.5×29.2 cm (18×11½ in.)

The Wilton Diptych is so called because it came to the National Gallery from Wilton House, home of the Earls of Pembroke in Wiltshire.

King Richard II, who was crowned in 1377 at the age of ten, deposed in 1399 and probably murdered in 1400, kneels in the left wing. He wears a collar of broomcods (pods of the broomplant) – livery of the kings of France – and a jewel of his own livery, the white hart. With him are Saint Edmund holding the arrow which killed him, Saint Edward holding a ring, and Saint John the Baptist in a camel skin. In the right wing stands the Virgin holding the Christ Child. Unusually the Child's halo is decorated with symbols of the Passion: the crown of thorns and three nails. With the Virgin and Child are eleven angels, each wearing a simpler collar of broomcods, and a white hart.

On the back are the royal arms (leopards and lilies), impaled with the arms of Edward the Confessor (choughs), and the white hart. On the basis of the heraldry the diptych has been dated around 1395, but the name of the artist is unknown.

2. Paolo Uccello (c.1397–1475)
The Battle of San Romano
Egg tempera on poplar, 181.6×320 cm (71½×126 in.)

This battle scene was probably painted in the 1450s. Together with its two companion paintings (now in the Louvre, Paris, and the Uffizi, Florence), it shows incidents from what was in fact a minor skirmish which took place between the Florentines and the Sienese in 1432. The victorious Florentines were led by Niccolò da Tolentino, seen here on a white charger at the centre, and identifiable by his device of the knot of Solomon, which is on the banner carried by the standard bearer behind him.

The three panels were probably commissioned by the Medici family, since they all came from the Medici (now Riccardi) Palace in Florence, where they were recorded on the death of Lorenzo the Magnificent in 1492.

Paolo Uccello was intensely interested in the newly discovered theory of one-point linear perspective, here demonstrated by the broken lances arranged artificially on the ground, and by mathematical foreshortening, as in the horses and Niccolò da Tolentino's hat. The total effect was intentionally highly decorative: the soldiers' armour is of silver leaf (now tarnished), the horses' harnesses are of gold leaf, and the background resembles a tapestry.

3. Jan van Eyck (active 1422; died 1441)
The Portrait of Giovanni (?) Arnolfini and Giovanna Cenami (?) ('The Arnolfini Marriage')

Oil on oak, 81.8×59.7 cm (32¼×23½ in.)

One of very few surviving full-length double portraits from the fifteenth century, this painting, dated 1434, is much more than a portrait. It is one of the most convincing representations of people within an interior from this period, and exemplifies van Eyck's skill in the depiction of light and his eye for meticulous detail. Light streams in from the window on the left, glancing off the brass chandelier and making the oranges near the window glow with colour. It also informs the painting of Giovanna Cenami's green dress, with its subtle range of tones, which van Eyck's oil painting technique permitted him to blend imperceptibly into one another.

The couple represented are thought to be an Italian merchant resident in Bruges, where van Eyck worked, and his wife. She is not pregnant, despite the bulk visible underneath her dress – her shape merely conforms to the prevailing idea of female beauty. Nor is the scene taking place in a bedroom: beds were commonly kept in many rooms in fifteenth-century houses. The painting is boldly inscribed in the centre in Latin 'Jan van Eyck was here', next to the mirror in which two more figures are reflected, entering the room. Although the painting certainly celebrates the marriage of the Arnolfini, it is far from certain that a marriage is taking place.

4. Piero della Francesca (active 1439; died 1492)
The Baptism of Christ
Egg tempera on poplar, 167×116 cm (66×45¾ in.)

The painting probably dates from the early 1450s, and is one of the earliest by Piero to have survived. It was painted for a chapel dedicated to Saint John in an abbey in Piero's native town of Borgo Sansepolcro and represents Saint John baptising his cousin Christ. The Holy Spirit, in the form of a dove, hovers above and heavenly light, in the form of fine lines of gold, falls down upon Christ's head as the water touches it. The angels attend with drapery to cover Christ. The clarity of the lighting, and of the volumes, seems inseparable from the stillness – or suspense – represented in the foreground. The landscape behind evokes the scenery around Borgo Sansepolcro.

The monumentality of Piero's style derived from his study in Florence of painters such as Masaccio. The lucidity of his compositions reminds us that he was also a notable mathematician.

5. Leonardo da Vinci (1452–1519)
The Virgin and Child with Saint John the Baptist and Saint Anne

Black and white chalk on tinted paper, 141.5×104.6 cm (55¾×41 in.)

The drawing represents the Virgin seated on the lap of her mother Saint Anne: they look at each other with pride and wonder as the infant Christ held by the Virgin greets his cousin Saint John, raising one hand in blessing and affectionately chucking his chin with the other.

The drawing is a full-size preparatory study for a painting commissioned by the King of France, which Leonardo eventually executed with a different composition. The study was probably made in about 1508, but Leonardo had been experimenting with this theme since about 1500. Some of the blurred and smudged effects of the drawing are deliberate; other parts were left in rough outline. Leonardo's famous painting of *The Virgin of the Rocks* in the National Gallery also depicts a meeting between the infant Christ and Saint John in a mysterious rocky setting, and there too parts of the composition have been left sketchy.

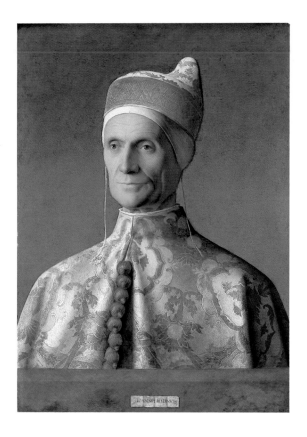

6. Giovanni Bellini (active *c.*1459; died 1516)
The Doge Leonardo Loredan

Oil on poplar, 61.5×45 cm (24¼×17¾ in.)

This painting of Doge Leonardo Loredan, ruler of the republican oligarchy of Venice, was probably made soon after his election in 1501. Bellini was then at the height of his powers. It is both the most admired portrait by him to have survived and perhaps the best preserved of all his known paintings. The features are immobile but the lips seem almost to smile and the eyes to move. Light animates all the surfaces, especially the gold thread on the damask, where the paint – almost certainly oil paint – is built up in relief.

If the picture is examined closely it will be seen that where the paint is thickest it is also roughly applied, not to represent form, but light. This way of handling paint was to be further developed by artists such as Titian.

7. Hans Holbein the Younger (1497/8–1543)
A Lady with a Squirrel and a Starling

Oil on oak, 56×38.8 cm (22×15¼ in.)

This portrait was painted in about 1527, during Holbein's first visit to England of 1526–8. The sitter has not yet been identified, though she is likely to have frequented the court of Henry VIII. The half-length format and blue background are characteristic of Holbein's English portraits, but the presence of two animals is unusual. A starling perches on a branch, and on the sitter's lap is a bright-eyed squirrel nibbling a nut. A chain around his neck shows he is a pet, but the presence of the starling is less easy to explain. It is possible that both animal and bird refer in some way to the sitter's name or coat of arms.

Holbein's portraits were usually worked up from drawings of the sitters. This is probably the case with this portrait, and it is unlikely that the starling or even the squirrel were present when the sitter posed for Holbein. Yet both animals and sitter are painted with Holbein's characteristically subtle attention to individualising details of outline and texture.

8. Titian (active by 1510; died 1576)
Bacchus and Ariadne

Oil on canvas, 175.2×190.5 cm (69×75 in.)

The painting illustrates two celebrated – and notably pictorial – passages of ancient poetry by Catullus and Ovid. Ariadne wanders barefoot and dishevelled by the shore of Dia, scanning the horizon for Theseus, the lover who has abandoned her. Bacchus, accompanied by his lewd and intoxicated train, chances upon her and offers her, as a wedding gift, the sky, in which she will be a constellation of stars. Then, fearing that she is alarmed by his leopards (Titian has painted cheetahs), Bacchus leaps from his chariot, embraces her, and bears her away.

The painting, which was completed in 1523, was commissioned for the small private studio of Duke Alfonso d'Este in his palace in Ferrara. It hung there together with Giovanni Bellini's *Feast of the Gods* (now in Washington, National Gallery of Art), and two other paintings by Titian (both now in the Prado), *The Worship of Venus* and *The Bacchanal of the Andrians*.

9. Peter Paul Rubens (1577–1640)
'Le Chapeau de Paille' ('The Straw Hat')
Oil on oak, 79×54 cm (31×21¼ in.)

This wide-eyed girl was probably Rubens's sister-in-law, Susanna Fourment, the daughter of an Antwerp silk and tapestry merchant. The occasion for the portrait may have been her marriage to Arnold Lunden in 1622. Her youngest sister, Hélène, became Rubens's second wife in 1630.

The picture was painted confidently and quickly. The paint is laid on with a freshness and energy which give the sitter a glowing vitality. The curling feathers of her hat, and the hair escaping from it, contribute to the feeling of spontaneity. The traditional title is inaccurate: the hat is felt, not straw.

Rubens worked for clients throughout Europe, among them Marie de Médicis, Philip IV of Spain and Charles I of England. He also served the Spanish Regents of the Netherlands as a diplomat, and it was in the dual role of diplomat and painter that he travelled to England in 1629, where he was knighted by the King.

10. Anthony van Dyck (1599–1641)
Equestrian Portrait of Charles I
Oil on canvas, 367×292 cm (144½×115 in.)

King Charles I was a small man with irregular features, but Van Dyck, the most famous of the King's court painters, always succeeded in making him look romantically handsome. In this portrait of about 1637, bare-headed, wearing Greenwich-made armour and mounted on a bay horse, the King rides out self-confidently in the countryside. The Latin inscription on the tablet which hangs on the tree at the right declares that he is Charles, King of Great Britain. The page below holds out the King's plumed helmet.

King Charles was an enthusiastic patron of the arts and the greatest collector to have occupied the throne. In addition to the present portrait, several paintings which he owned are now in the National Gallery, including Rubens's *Peace and War* and Correggio's *School of Love*. He persuaded Van Dyck to move to London in 1632, and until his early death in 1641 Van Dyck was in constant demand as a portraitist to the royal family and members of the court.

11. Diego Velázquez (1599–1660)
The Toilet of Venus ('The Rokeby Venus')

Oil on canvas, 122.5×177 cm (48¼×69¾ in.)

This is the only survivor of four female nudes painted by Velázquez and is thus unique in Spanish seventeenth-century art. It is also one of the most haunting images of female beauty in western painting. Made around the time of Velázquez's second visit to Italy in 1649 the painting is also unusual in showing Venus from behind, stretched out luxuriously on a bed covered with rich silks. The mirror held by her son, a plump Cupid, gives only the vaguest of reflections, indicating that the artist did not intend her face to be the prime object of our interest. Indeed the viewer's attention is constantly brought back to the pale, clear body of the goddess, beautifully drawn and modelled with paint of the subtlest colours.

Given the religious climate in Spain during the seventeenth century, painting nude women was not a common occupation for artists: the depiction of naked bodies, both male and female, was frowned upon by the Inquisition. However, the royal collection, to which Velázquez had access and for which he painted, had several paintings of nudes, including the group of famous paintings by Titian. Although these paintings must have inspired Velázquez, the composition of the 'Rokeby Venus' (so called because it hung at Rokeby Hall in Yorkshire) is entirely his own invention.

12. Rembrandt (1606–1669)
Self Portrait aged 63

Oil on canvas, 86×70 cm (33⅞×27¾ in.)

Painted in the last year of his life, this self portrait shows the artist tired and battered by illness and misfortune. He had already suffered the loss of his wife, his mistress and his son, and experienced a period of financial difficulty. In this picture the careful modelling and tight descriptive brushwork of his earlier paintings have given way to bold, heavy brushstrokes and broad application of the palette knife. Attention is concentrated on the face and to a lesser extent the hands.

Rembrandt's self portraits, of which some sixty survive today, are unique in seventeenth-century painting. The artist's face was remarkably expressive and he used himself as his own model in his restless search for new ways of representing the emotions. Many artists have observed the process of ageing, but few have expressed it with greater poignancy than Rembrandt.

13. Claude Gellée (Le Lorrain) (1604/5–1682)
Landscape with Psyche outside the Palace of Cupid
('The Enchanted Castle')

Oil on canvas, 87×151 cm (34¼×59½ in.)

Claude was from Lorraine but worked mainly in Rome, where he specialised in painting poetic visions of nature often inspired by the writers of antiquity. The subject-matter of this picture, painted in 1664 for the Roman aristocrat Lorenzo Colonna, derives generally from the story of Psyche as told by Apuleius in the *Golden Ass*, but the precise incident is unclear. It shows Psyche, possibly after her abandonment by her lover, Cupid, or possibly contemplating her future before she has met him. At all events, the building in the background represents Cupid's castle. Its architecture, with no obvious exits or entrances and its unlit windows, together with Psyche's solitude and Claude's use of light, combine to give the painting its mysterious effect. By not defining precisely time or place, Claude allows space for the viewer's imagination to participate in enhancing the mystery.

Itself inspired by a literary source, Claude's painting, dubbed 'The Enchanted Castle' in the late eighteenth century, may well have been one of the inspirations for Keats's 'Ode to a Nightingale', written in 1820.

14. Johannes Vermeer (1632–1675)
A Young Woman standing at a Virginal

Oil on canvas, 51.7×45.2 cm (20½×17⅞ in.)

Vermeer, who lived and worked in Delft, was the greatest of all Dutch painters of genre subjects, that is, scenes based on everyday life. In this picture, the standing young woman may be intended to represent fidelity. But, whatever the particular associations, Vermeer's real subject is light and its transforming effects upon the surfaces on which it falls. The painting of Cupid on the wall appears in at least one other painting by Vermeer and has been attributed to Cesar van Everdingen.

In paintings from the end of his career, such as this one and its possible pair, *A Young Woman seated at a Virginal*, also in the National Gallery, the surface is of an almost porcelain smoothness and the highlights have become touches of pure pigment. Both paintings were once in the collection of the French critic Théophile Thoré, whose series of articles on Vermeer in the *Gazette des Beaux-Arts* in 1888 did much to reawaken interest in the painter.

15. Canaletto (1697–1768)
'The Stonemason's Yard'

Oil on canvas, 123.8×162.9 cm (48¾×64⅛ in.)

The picture is more intimate than many of Canaletto's paintings, especially those he made for the aristocratic British tourists in Venice. Canaletto shows us an ordinary campo (or open space) which has been temporarily transformed into a makeshift workshop where large blocks of stone could be unloaded from the canal and carved: they would then have been attached to the church of San Vidal, which was receiving a new façade during the 1720s when this painting was made. The church itself is not visible: in fact Canaletto must have had his back to it in order to see this view – although as in most of Canaletto's work the view depicted is never exactly what can be seen.

The painting is one of the few views of Venice where we are able to observe a normal working morning where people go about their chores: spinning, gathering water from a well (a well which still exists), hanging out the washing and coping with naughty children. All this goes on around the men who chip away at the stones, tools casually strewn around their work area. The fresh early morning sunlight casts strong shadows across the scene: and as the clouds of the night's rains are blown away, the painting is filled with the promise of the beautiful warm day ahead.

16. Joseph Mallord William Turner (1775–1851)
The 'Fighting Temeraire' tugged to her Last Berth to be broken up, 1838

Oil on canvas, 90.8×121.9 cm (35¾×48 in.)

The 'Temeraire' was launched in 1798 and fought bravely at the Battle of Trafalgar in 1805, when she acquired the popular name given in Turner's title. On 28 September 1838 the ship was towed up the Thames from Sheerness to the ship-breaking yard at Rotherhithe.

Turner is said to have been a witness to the scene and to have made quick sketches on the spot, but the finished painting is not intended as a detailed record of the event. Turner used the combination of a spectacular sunset with the imminent end of the old ship to evoke feelings of nostalgia and loss.

The highly atmospheric use of colour and the concern with generalised effects rather than with specific detail make the ship seem almost a part of the natural world. By contrast, the dark sharply outlined silhouette of the tugboat's funnel draws attention to the arrival of modern technology, a change with which Turner was much preoccupied. Here steam replaces sail; his response to the new steam railways was expressed in another of his paintings in the National Gallery, *Rain, Steam and Speed – The Great Western Railway.*

17. John Constable (1776–1837)
The Hay Wain

Oil on canvas, 130.2×185.4 cm (51¼×73 in.)

Constable himself first titled this picture 'Landscape: Noon', but it was given its better known name by a friend. The painting shows a scene in Constable's native Suffolk. On the left is the cottage rented by the farmer Willy Lott, and in the centre a farm-wagon – the hay wain of the title – crosses the Flatford mill-stream at a ford near the River Stour.

Constable painted a series of six large pictures based on the scenery around the River Stour, of which this is one. Although studies taken directly from nature – especially of the sky – played an important part in such works, Constable also drew on his own paintings, as well as on those of seventeenth-century Dutch painters.

The painting was well received when it was shown at the Royal Academy in 1821. It also made a profound impression on the contemporary French painters Géricault and Delacroix when it was exhibited at the Salon in Paris. Delacroix subsequently adopted Constable's technique of using small dabs of colour to suggest the effects of swiftly changing light.

18. Jean-Auguste-Dominique Ingres (1780–1867)
Madame Moitessier

Oil on canvas, 120×92 cm (47¼×36¼ in.)

This is one of a series of brilliant society portraits painted by Ingres in the 1840s and 1850s. An inscription on the frame of the mirror records that the painting was completed in 1856 when the artist was 76 years old, yet this simple statement belies the effort and anxieties that went into its production. The portrait was commissioned some twelve years earlier, in 1844, and in the course of its execution Ingres altered the composition several times. The costume, for example, was changed at least three times – in the final picture Madame Moitessier wears a floral dress, supported by the wide-hooped crinolines which were fashionable in the mid-1850s. The elaborate clothes and the expensive accessories help to create a suitable image for the wife of a wealthy banker. However, the distinctive pose with the hand held against the cheek is based on a personification of Arcadia in a Roman fresco from Herculaneum, which Ingres may have seen at the museum in Naples.

   In this polished and refined portrait with its idealised forms and perfect outlines, Madame Moitessier is presented as a modern goddess whose classical beauty and dignity transcend the wealth and materialism of a Second Empire drawing room.

19. Claude Monet (1840–1926)
Bathers at La Grenouillère

Oil on canvas, 73×92 cm (28¾×36¼ in.)

During the summer of 1869 Monet worked with Renoir at La Grenouillère, a café and bathing place on the banks of an island in the Seine near Bougival. This was a popular venue for a day trip from Paris and the atmosphere was relaxed and colourful. In a letter to his friend Bazille, Monet declared his ambition to produce a picture of La Grenouillère, for which so far he had made only 'a few bad sketches'.

The National Gallery painting and a work of similar dimensions in the Metropolitan Museum in New York are probably the 'bad sketches' referred to by Monet. His final picture has not survived but, despite the artist's disparaging comments, the studies are now recognised as important milestones in the history of Impressionism. Working in the open air, Monet painted at great speed, applying the paint with broad strokes and dabs to suggest the movement of the rippling water and the constantly shifting boats and their reflections. Patches of vivid, pure colours help to evoke the dazzling appearance of bright, outdoor light.

The informal composition, the sketch-like techniques and, above all, the qualities of directness and spontaneity that are apparent in this work were to form the basis of the Impressionist style evolved by Monet and his colleagues over the following years.

20. Georges Seurat (1859–1891)
Bathers at Asnières

Oil on canvas, 201×300 cm (79⅛×118⅛ in.)

This picture, which was rejected by the Paris Salon of 1884 and exhibited instead at the newly founded Salon des Indépendants, is Seurat's first major large-scale composition. The subject of bathers by the Seine was common in Impressionist pictures, and both Monet and Renoir had worked at this suburb to the north-west of Paris. Seurat produced numerous small open-air oil sketches of the site, but the finished work shows little interest in fleeting effects of light and atmosphere. It is an elaborate, studio composition and the details of the poses and costumes were worked out in a series of careful drawings. The bathers are solidly defined and arranged in a static group, like an antique frieze.

Although Seurat had yet to develop his technique of painting with spots of bright colour, there are areas in the picture which look forward to his rigorous and systematic style known as 'divisionism' – the red tones of the hat worn by the boy on the right, for example, are painted over with dots of orange and blue.

The National
Gallery Main Floor

The Staircase at the Orange Street
Entrance leads to Lower Floor Gallery
A. Galleries B – F are accessible via the
staircase in Room 13

♿ Orange Street Entrance

toilet
also for
disabled
visitors

Lifts

22
21
20

23
22a
19

24
25

26
27

18
17
16

28

14
11
5
3

The Sunley
Room
12
13
Lift
Board
Room

10
9
The Wohl
Room
8

6
4
2
7

Central
Hall

Shop

Lift

29
30

32
37
36
40
44

38
39

35
34

33

45
46

43
42

41

Link
Lifts

51
60
61

52
59
62

53
58
63

54
57
64

55
56
65
66

Trafalgar Square Entrance

♿ Sainsbury Wing